Herefordsh

The pastoral landscape of Herefordshire, with its broad plains set between hills, its sparkling rivers and its delightful architecture, has much to offer the visitor. Once a turbulent area of border raids and skirmishes, the county is now better known for its tranquil villages steeped in history and its bustling market towns. From its black-and-white "magpie" cottages and houses to its historic cathedral and ancient castles, Herefordshire has a rich heritage of impressive buildings, while the gently rolling hills and the beautiful valleys of the River Wye, the River Dore and the little River Arrow provide some of the finest rural scenery in the country.

SALMON

Herefordshire

A rural county of great beauty, Herefordshire is known for its rolling hills, its cider apple orchards and the grazing meadows which line its many rivers. Two river valleys provide some of Herefordshire's finest scenery: the Wye Valley in the south of the county and the River Dore in the west, which meanders along the "Golden Valley" of cornfields, orchards and rich pastureland. Herefordshire is also known for its hop fields. A native plant long before it began to be cultivated in the 16th century for flavouring beer, hops still flourish in Herefordshire. Ripening in late summer, they can often be seen twining their way up 12-14 feet high hop poles or strings.

There is a long tradition of working on the land in Herefordshire where agriculture has been the principal occupation for many centuries. The distinctive, heavily-built **Hereford cattle**, with their curly red coats and white faces, are a familiar sight across the county. The breed originated in the Welsh borders, but its hardiness makes it very adaptable and it is now widespread throughout the country. Herefordshire cattle are renowned for producing some of the finest and leanest beef in the world.

A rich fruit-growing area, Herefordshire's climate and soil are particularly suited to the growing of cider apples. The county has long been famous for its cider and, traditionally, each small farm and many cottages had an orchard from which they produced their own brew. Nowadays, larger, more commercial fruit farms are taking over, and in spring much of the county is covered with blossom. The Museum of Cider in Hereford, which tells the history of cider-making through the ages, has a fascinating collection of old machinery used by cider makers such as presses, vats and bottle-washing machines.

Historic Hereford

A city steeped in history, **Hereford** was the capital of the kingdom of West Mercia in Saxon times, a walled city with a fine defensive castle. Both the city and cathedral were founded about 700 AD and many outstanding buildings from past centuries have been preserved. At the heart of Hereford is High Town, which was the Saxon market centre of the city. As well as its market hall and shops, High Town contains many attractive 17th and 18th century buildings.

The six arches of the handsome, 15th century **Old Wye Bridge** span the River Wye just upstream from the cathedral. A well-preserved section of the ancient city wall can still be seen near the river. Somewhat newer is the handsome **Victoria Suspension Bridge** which links Castle Green with Bishop's Meadow and King George's Fields.

Behind the cathedral lie the pleasant **Redcliffe Gardens**. Providing a peaceful oasis in the centre of the town, the gardens slope away from the cathedral and meet the river where it runs between Wye Bridge and Castle Green.

The picturesque half-timbered **Old House**, which dates from 1621, is an outstanding example of Jacobean domestic architecture. Now housing a museum, it was originally built as a residence for a master builder, and is the sole survivor of a row of houses which were known as Butcher's Row.

The glory of the city of Hereford is undoubtedly its 11th century **cathedral** which occupies a picturesque setting on the banks of the River Wye. Although it is relatively small, it is one of the finest of Britain's cathedrals. Dating mainly from Norman times, the present cathedral buildings reflect the many changes which have occurred through the centuries. The massive central tower dates from around 1325 and the splendid west front was also originally built in the 14th century, although it was restored in the late 1700s. The cathedral also has an impressive array of monuments and brasses which is unrivalled by any other English cathedral. Pre-eminent among the cathedral's treasures is the outstanding medieval chained library, the largest of its kind in the world. It contains some 1500 books, each fastened to the oak bookcases by an individual chain.

The collection includes a version of the Gospels dating from the eighth century, a number of 13th and 14th century manuscripts and two volumes by William Caxton, the 15th century pioneer of printing in England. Another of Hereford's treasures is a *mappa mundi*, which dates from 1289. Drawn on vellum, this is the largest complete example of a map depicting the world as it was known at that time.

Hereford cathedral is particularly known for its Lady Chapel and its magnificent Norman nave. The vaulting was replaced in the 18th century during restoration work after the collapse of the western tower. Massive pink sandstone columns line the nave which has a feeling of great spaciousness and light.

Along the River Wye

South of Hereford the beautiful **River Wye** winds serenely towards Ross-on-Wye, flanked by grazing meadows and surrounded by magnificent rolling countryside, much of which is recognised as an Area of Outstanding Natural Beauty. In places thickly wooded, dotted with pretty villages and offering superb views, the Wye Valley has inspired many great writers including Wordsworth, Shaw and poet Thomas Gray. The pretty village of **Mordiford** *(top)*, which lies in the heart of Herefordshire's cider-making country, is situated at the point where the River Lugg meets the River Wye. This is an ancient crossing point, and the present nine-arched bridge dates from the 14th century. Among the other delightful villages which are found along this part of the river valley are **Hampton Bishop** *(bottom)*, and **Fownhope** *(centre)*, both on the east bank of the river. Hampton Bishop is rich in the black and white cottages which are typical of the area, and even the church has a half-timbered tower. St. Mary's Church at Fownhope is large and impressive with a fine Norman tower supporting a 15th century shingled oak spire.

The Church of All Saints at **Brockhampton** is a remarkable building which, contrary to its appearance, dates only from the early 1900s. With its thatched roof and lych-gate, the church was designed in medieval style by followers of William Morris and the Arts & Crafts Movement. It has unusually steep arches in the nave, and contains a tapestry designed by Sir Edwin Burne-Jones as well as some fine 20th century stained glass. Among its older treasures are two altar pieces, one Flemish and one Italian in origin.

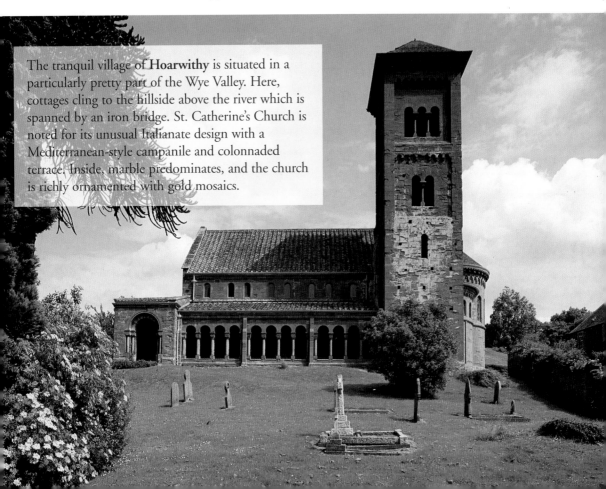

The tranquil village of **Hoarwithy** is situated in a particularly pretty part of the Wye Valley. Here, cottages cling to the hillside above the river which is spanned by an iron bridge. St. Catherine's Church is noted for its unusual Italianate design with a Mediterranean-style campanile and colonnaded terrace. Inside, marble predominates, and the church is richly ornamented with gold mosaics.

Ross-on-Wye

The historic market town of **Ross-on-Wye** stands high on a sandstone cliff overlooking a wide loop of the river. It is an excellent centre for exploring the beautiful Wye Valley, which is one of the most picturesque areas of Britain. Many fine Georgian and earlier houses line the steep streets of the town which is famous as the birthplace in 1637 of local benefactor John Kyrle. Immortalised by Alexander Pope in his *Moral Essays* as the "Man of Ross", he was responsible for giving the town a public water supply, and for laying out the attractive Prospect Gardens near the church. From the gardens there are magnificent views of the river and of the hills, stretching away westwards into Wales.

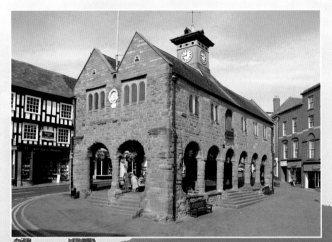

Ross-on-Wye was at one time a busy coaching town, which is reflected in its charming old inns and splendid **Market Hall**. This handsome building was erected in the late 17th century to replace an earlier market hall, and is now listed as an ancient monument.

The road from Ross-on-Wye to Goodrich crosses the Wye at **Wilton Bridge** which was built in 1599 at the site of an existing ford. It incorporates some intricate, indented stonework and there is a quaint four-square stone sundial surmounting a pillar.

Dominating the skyline, the 208 feet high spire of **St. Mary's Church** is a notable local landmark. Beautifully proportioned, with two aisles, chancel and chapel, the church was founded in the reign of King Stephen, although most of the present structure dates from the 14th century. In the churchyard there is a Plague Cross, commemorating the terrible plague of 1637.

Around Symonds Yat

At Symonds Yat the River Wye meanders through a narrow, tree-hung gorge creating a huge loop around the foot of 473 feet high **Yat Rock**. From the summit of this wooded outcrop there is a majestic prospect across the Herefordshire countryside which is one of the best-known views in the Wye Valley. The calm progress of the river is interrupted at Symonds Yat by a series of rapids, small islands and limestone outcrops which all help to create a scene of great beauty.

Below Symonds Yat, where two river-side inns stand beside the river, there is an ancient crossing point where a ferry has long carried passengers from one bank to the other. *The Olde Ferrie Inn* and *The Saracen's Head* still offer a welcome stopping place for travellers.

The **Log Cabin** is a pleasant place to stop and enjoy the woodland scenery. From here a waymarked path twists and turns downhill through the trees towards the river.

Impressively situated on a sandstone outcrop overlooking the River Wye, **Goodrich Castle** is pre-eminent among Herefordshire's border fortresses. It was begun in the 12th century to guard the strategic river crossing into Wales, and was later extended. Although it was impregnable on two sides due to the cliffs rising from the river bank, and protected on the landward side by a man-made moat hewn from the rock, the fortress was successfully besieged in 1326 and subsequently destroyed by Parliamentary troops during the Civil War.

Historic Ledbury

The attractive market town of Ledbury abounds in outstanding examples of Elizabethan architecture, among them the superb 16th century **Feathers Hotel**. The magnificent Tudor timbering was at one time hidden behind a covering of plaster. It was restored to its original impressive state at the end of the 19th century.

The historic **Market House** which stands in Ledbury's main street is one of the most outstanding black-and-white buildings in the area. Supported on sixteen solid pillars of Spanish chestnut, it was built in 1633 by John Abel who was dubbed "King's Carpenter" in recognition of his work in the service of King Charles I.

Standing on the western slopes of the Malvern Hills near Ledbury is the beautiful old village of **Eastnor**. Here there are a number of superb thatched and timber-framed cottages which are typical of the domestic architecture of the area.

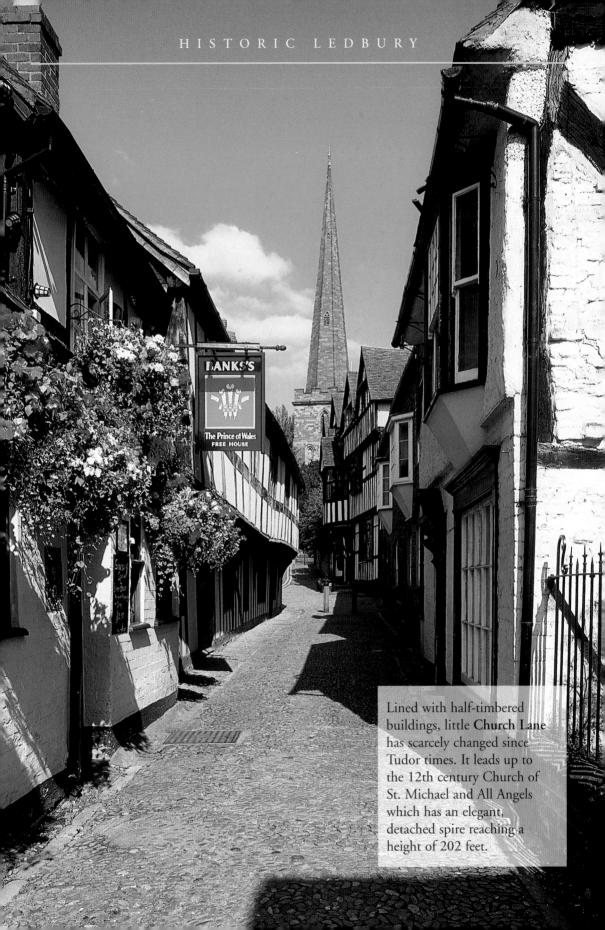

Lined with half-timbered buildings, little **Church Lane** has scarcely changed since Tudor times. It leads up to the 12th century Church of St. Michael and All Angels which has an elegant, detached spire reaching a height of 202 feet.

Bromyard and the Malverns

The ancient market town of **Bromyard** lies in the valley of the River Frome. It has been an important local centre since before the Domesday survey and among its heritage of fine buildings are the 16th century Bridge House and the half-timbered Falcon Hotel, an old coaching inn.

The Bromyard Art Trail takes in several works of art which were specially commissioned in 2000 to explore the town's history in the context of the new Millennium. The **Time Tower** imitates the timber-framed structure of many local buildings and is decorated with carvings based on Bromyard's agricultural heritage. Among these are chickens, rabbits, vegetables, cider apples and hops.

St. Peter's Church dates from the 12th century and retains some of its Norman features. There is an unusual castellated exterior turret to the tower and above the south doorway is a carving of St. Peter carrying the keys of the Kingdom. The beautiful east window depicts the risen Christ surrounded by saints, prophets and martyrs, all entwined in the branches of a vine.

The Herefordshire Beacon rises to a height of 1,114 feet and on it are the extensive remains of the Iron Age **British Camp**. It covers some forty-four acres and its concentric ramparts are nearly two miles in circumference.

The Black and White Villages

Leominster is the starting point of the Black and White Village Trail. About forty miles in length, this circular route takes in many of the delightful black-and-white villages of north-west Herefordshire. These are some of the most attractive and unspoiled villages in all England, known for their splendid timber-framed buildings and ancient churches. **Dilwyn**, some five miles from Leominster, has a number of black-and-white houses and cottages grouped around the green. The Church of St. Mary the Virgin, which dates from the 13th century, has a Norman west tower surmounted by an 18th century spire.

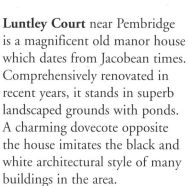

Luntley Court near Pembridge is a magnificent old manor house which dates from Jacobean times. Comprehensively renovated in recent years, it stands in superb landscaped grounds with ponds. A charming dovecote opposite the house imitates the black and white architectural style of many buildings in the area.

Eardisley is an outstandingly pretty village which retains many interesting historic features in addition to the delightful black-and-white houses which line its single street. A fine Norman border castle once stood here but, after being repeatedly attacked during border skirmishes, it was finally destroyed in the Civil War. The Church of St. Mary Magdalene also dates from Norman times and retains an intriguing 12th century cup-shaped font, decorated with remarkable high-relief carvings.

None of Herefordshire's black-and-white villages is more beautiful than **Weobley**, which can trace its origins back to the 7th century. The prosperity which came through its industries of glove and ale making is reflected in the abundance of fine timber-framed houses and inns, some of them dating from the early 1300s. They radiate out from the main street beneath the slender spire of the Church of St. Peter and St. Paul.

Kington is one of several attractive market towns in Herefordshire and the impressive Market Hall testifies to its former importance. Surrounded by fine hill-walking country, Kington is essentially a border town. It lies on Offa's Dyke, the defensive barrier built between England and Wales by King Offa of Mercia in the 8th century.

Historic Pembridge

In the unspoilt village of **Pembridge**, almost every building is a superb example of its kind. Each is a delight to the eye, whether it is a well-preserved medieval house with leaded windows and irregular roof, a charming riverside cottage of timber, brick and stone, or a handsome building which served as manor house or school house in Tudor and Stuart times.

Some fine half-timbered cottages and inns are clustered around the triangular market place and nearby stands the splendid Market Hall, which dates from the early 1500s.

Among the other outstanding buildings in Pembridge is St. Mary's Church, which dates from the mid-14th century. It possesses an unusual detached wooden belfry which was used as a place of refuge for villagers when the Welsh carried out raids across the border. It is one of seven similar detached towers which can be found in the county.

Picturesque Eardisland

With its delightful setting on the tranquil River Arrow, **Eardisland** is known for its wealth of remarkable timber and plaster buildings. The village grew up around the Norman castle which was built to protect the route between England and Wales. Today, all that remains of the castle is a tree-covered mound, situated between the river and the church. St. Mary's dates mainly from the early 13th century, but the tower was rebuilt in 1728 after the collapse of the original one. Successfully combining the old and the new, a splendid modern stained glass window incorporates in its design a typical black and white Eardisland house.

The little **River Arrow**, spanned by an old stone bridge, flows gently past Eardisland's ancient cottages. One of the principal tributaries of the River Wye, the River Arrow flows through tranquil farming country rich in wildlife. Here it is possible to see many different species of birds while badgers, foxes and hares are also found in the valley.

Historic Houses and Gardens

Standing on the western slopes of the Malvern Hills near Ledbury, the beautiful old village of Eastnor is known for its superb thatched and timber-framed cottages. **Eastnor Castle** is a magnificent Georgian mansion built in medieval style. The ornate Italianate and Gothic interior has been splendidly restored. The grounds include a deer park, a lake and a fine arboretum which contains many mature specimens of both broad-leaved trees and conifers.

Dinmore Manor, with its fine chapel and music room, stands in superb gardens some six miles north of Hereford. The house itself is largely 16th century but in the grounds, detached from the house, is a Chapel of the Knights Hospitalers of St. John of Jerusalem which dates from the 12th to the 14th century. A stone bridge adds a focal point to the delightful gardens.

Lower Brockhampton, near Bromyard, is a splendid example of a half-timbered manor house. Dating mainly from the 14th century, it has an exceptionally well-preserved gatehouse over the moat, and the ruins of a 12th century chapel can also be seen. Built for a squire's son, this substantial homestead has a picturesque buckled roof of fine old tiles and a galleried dining-hall.

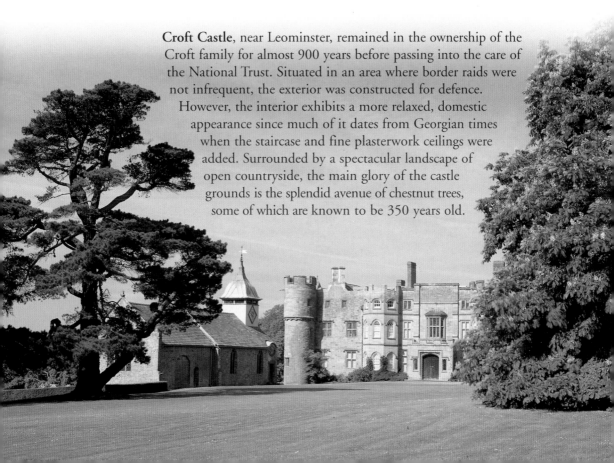

Croft Castle, near Leominster, remained in the ownership of the Croft family for almost 900 years before passing into the care of the National Trust. Situated in an area where border raids were not infrequent, the exterior was constructed for defence. However, the interior exhibits a more relaxed, domestic appearance since much of it dates from Georgian times when the staircase and fine plasterwork ceilings were added. Surrounded by a spectacular landscape of open countryside, the main glory of the castle grounds is the splendid avenue of chestnut trees, some of which are known to be 350 years old.

Set in eleven acres incorporating a medieval church, **How Caple Court** occupies a superb situation in a tree-lined valley overlooking a bend in the River Wye upstream of Ross-on-Wye. The intriguing garden combines formal terraces, a restored Florentine garden and a pool with an unusual pergola. The Edwardian planting scheme has recently been re-established to great effect.

The gardens of **Hergest Croft**, near Kington, are famous for their trees and shrubs. Azaleas and rhododendrons make a colourful display in summer, and in autumn the rich tints of the maples and birch trees are particularly striking. A family home for more than one hundred years, the lay-out and planting of the garden have been influenced by the writings of well-known garden designers William Robinson and Gertrude Jekyll.

Leominster

The attractive old market town of **Leominster** has a great variety of impressive architecture, much of it resulting from the prosperity which came with the wool trade. The local Ryelands sheep produced wool of exceptional quality, and for five hundred years the town was famous for its fine-spun Lemster Ore. Among many outstanding buildings in the town is **Grange Court**, a splendid example of half-timbered work dating from 1633. It was originally built as a Market Hall or Buttercross, and moved from its original site to its present location in the 19th century.

According to tradition, the 12th century Benedictine Priory at Leominster was founded by Leofric, Earl of Mercia and husband of Lady Godiva. Most of the buildings disappeared after the priory was dissolved in 1539, but the **Priory Church**, dedicated to St. Peter and St. Paul, is still used as the parish church. It is remarkable for possessing three naves, the earliest of which is an outstanding example of early Norman work. Within the church many intriguing features and artifacts are preserved, among them a rare medieval paten and chalice.

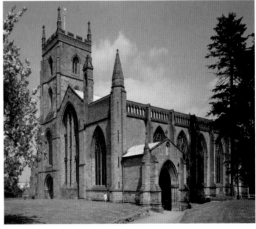

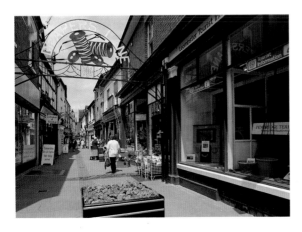

From the Middle Ages, Leominster was a major commercial centre dominated by eight powerful medieval guilds, and the centre of the town is criss-crossed by fascinating little lanes which are a reminder of that time. Draping is an old English term for weaving, hence **Drapers Lane**, now lined with a variety of intriguing shops, was once the street where weavers plied their trade.

The Golden Valley

Known for centuries as the "**Golden Valley**", a beautiful stretch of the River Dore valley winds for ten miles from Dorstone to Pontrilas. Flanked in the west by the Black Mountains, the river flows

through the orchards, cornfields and meadows which constitute some of Herefordshire's finest scenery. In the quiet village of Abbey Dore, at the southern end of the valley, stands **Dore Abbey.** Founded in 1147, it is a fine example of Early English architecture, although the tower was added in the 17th century during reconstruction work. Dore Abbey is unique in that it is the only instance where the chancel and transepts of a Cistercian abbey are in current use as a parish church.

At the head of the Golden Valley is the historic village of Dorstone. Overlooking the village from its position on the ridge stands **Arthur's Stone**, a burial chamber which dates from about 3000 BC. The huge, twenty feet long capstone, supported by upright stones, which is now a well-known local landmark, served as the entrance to a large oval chamber.

Built within a hundred years of the Norman conquest, tiny **Kilpeck Church** is one of the finest Norman churches remaining in Britain. Dedicated to St. Mary and St. David, this outstanding example of Norman workmanship is particularly noted for its richly decorated south doorway which is ornamented with symbolic carvings of mythical beasts, angels and devils. Among other interesting features of the church are the west window, the bell turret, and a remarkable Saxon stoup.

The church at **St. Margarets**, another delightful Golden Valley village, is notable for its remarkable lace-work wooden screen.

Eardisland

Leominster

River Arrow

Kington

Pembridge

Dilwyn

Weobley

Eardisley

Bromyard

Stretton Grandison

River Lugg

River Wye

River Frome

Malvern
Hills

Dorstone

Hampton Bishop

Ledbury

Hereford

Mordiford

Eastnor

St. Margarets

Golden Valley

Fownhope

Brockhampton

Abbey Dore

Kilpeck

Hoarwithy

Pontrilas

Ross-on-Wye

Goodrich

Symonds Yat

Front Cover: Hereford, Symonds Yat, Ledbury and Ross-on-Wye.
Title Page: River Wye at Symonds Yat.
Inside Back Cover: The Olde Ferrie Inn, Symonds Yat.
Back Cover: Herefordshire cottage at Eastnor.

Printed and published by J. Salmon Ltd.,
100 London Road, Sevenoaks, Kent TN13 1BB.
Copyright © 2002 J. Salmon Ltd. All rights reserved.
ISBN 1-902842-23-5